ABOUT ALL AFRICAN STATES AND PEOPLE

BABY PROFESSOR

EDUCATION KIDS

Speedy Publishing LLC
40 E. Main St. #1156
Newark, DE 19711
www.speedypublishing.com

Copyright 2016

Learn about

AFRICA

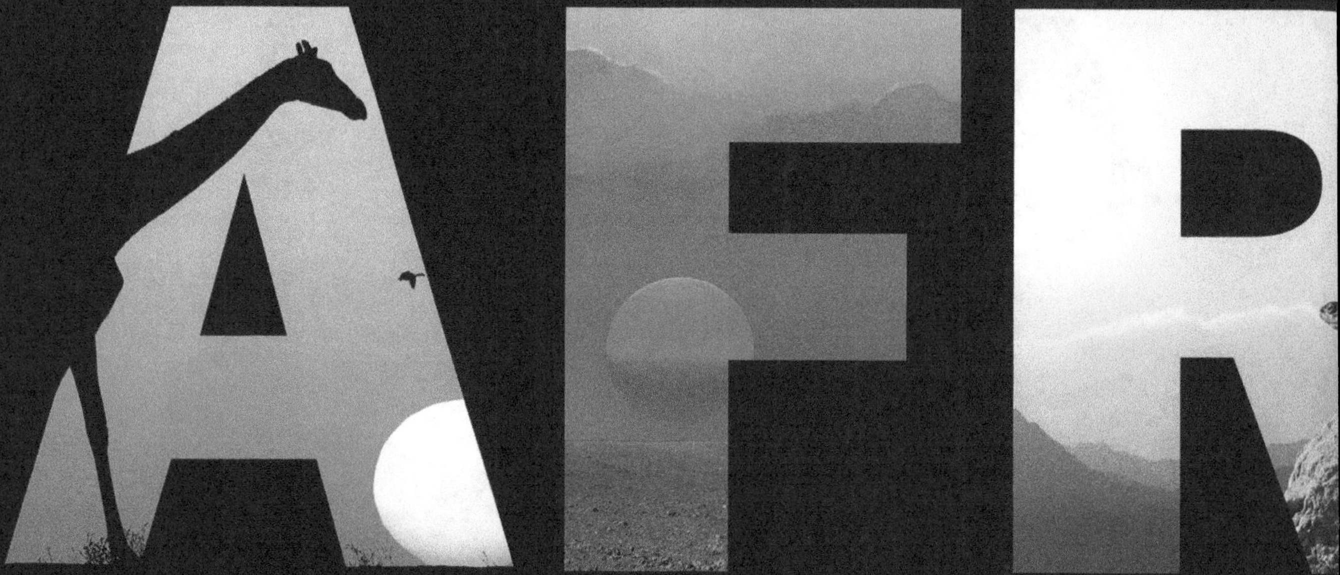
AFR

The first humans, and the first civilizations, began in Africa. The Pharaonic civilization of ancient Egypt is one of the world's oldest and longest-lasting civilizations. Cave paintings have been found in South Africa that are over 75,000 years old.

Long before humans emerged, Africa was attached to all the other continents to form one massive landmass called Pangea. Over millions of years Pangea slowly broke apart to form the world's continents as we know them today.

INENTAL DRIFT

AFTER

Arctic ocean

NORTH
AMERICA

EURASIA

Atlantic
ocean

Pacific
ocean

AFRICA

SOUTH
AMERICA

Indian
ocean

Southern ocean

ANTARCTICA

ys
an

Lucy is the common name
of AL 288-1. A female
of the hominin species
Australopithecus afarensis.

The oldest human remains discovered so far were found in Ethiopia. The remains are roughly 200,000 years old. Africa is the world's oldest populated area. Africa is where human beings first appeared on earth.

Africa has the most countries of any continent. It has 54 countries and one non-self governing territory, the Western Sahara. It is the second largest and second most heavily populated continent.

Almost all of Africa was colonized by European powers during the 18th and 19th centuries, except Ethiopia and Liberia. Before colonial rule, Africa had up to 10,000 different states and autonomous groups with distinct languages and customs.

Today, Africa is united under a political organization known as the African Union (AU). The AU was established in 2001. Only Morocco is not a member of the AU.

One quarter of the world's languages are spoken only in Africa, with over 2,000 documented languages. South Africa is called the "Rainbow Nation" partly because it has 11 official languages spoken by people of many different races.

Islam is the dominant religion in Africa. Christianity is the second largest. Arabic is the most widely-spoken language. By 2050, about 38% of all the world's Christians will be living in Sub-Saharan Africa (SSA).

Half of all Africans are under the age of 25. Almost 40% of adults in Africa are illiterate and two-thirds of the population are women. The continent's population will double to 2.3 billion people by 2050.

Over 25 million people on Africa are HIV-positive and 17 million have died of AIDS. One in four adults in Swaziland is infected with HIV. Almost 90% of all cases of malaria worldwide occur in Africa.

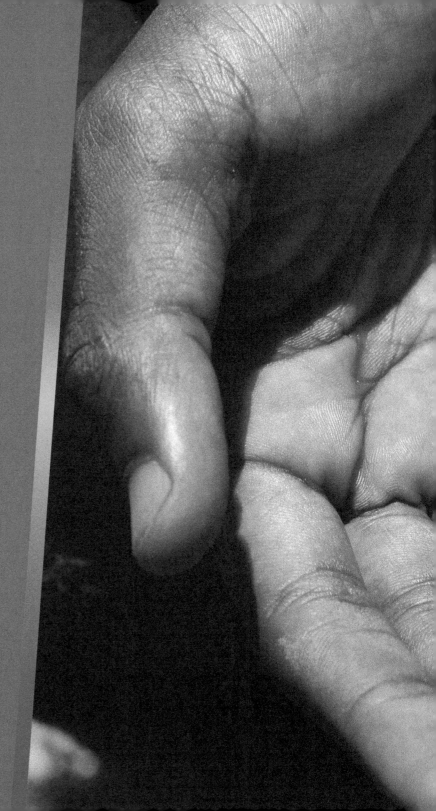

Here are some interesting facts in Africa. Tanzania has the world's highest Albinism. Women from Africa's Mursi tribe pierce their lips and wear plates as large as five inches across. A lone tribe in Kenya-called the "Kalenjin" has the fastest long-distance runners in the world.

More people speak French in Africa than there are people in France. The most popular sports in Africa are soccer and cricket. Both sports were introduced during the colonial era. Timbuktu, Mali is home of one of the oldest universities in the world, established in 982 CE.

In Africa, people have to walk an average of 3.7 miles daily to fetch water for various uses. About 41% of children in Africa aged between 5-10 years are actively involved in child labor. In Burundi, 39% of infants and toddler are underweight.

Africa is one of the most diverse places on the planet with a wide variety of terrain, wildlife, and climates. Its major natural areas are desert, savanna, and rain forest. Africa is full of natural beauty.

Africa is home to the world's largest living land animals, the African elephant and the giraffe. The hippopotamus is Africa's deadliest animal. Africa is rich with wildlife, including penguins, vultures, lions, cheetahs, seals, giraffes, gorillas, and crocodiles.

Giraffe by now
are extinct in
at least seven
countries in
Africa. There are
no wild tigers
in Africa, only
in Asia. The
hippopotamus
kills more
African people
than do
crocodiles and
lions combined.

The fastest land animal in the world, the cheetah, lives in Africa. It is also a home to the world's largest reptile, the Nile crocodile. The world's largest primate, the gorilla, can also be found in the jungles of Africa.

Just as the people of Africa are diverse, so are the fish. Lake Malawi has more different fish species than any other freshwater system on earth. Africa's Lake Malawi has more than 500 varieties of fish.

Cairo is Africa's largest city. It is Egypt's capital and Egypt is Africa's most popular tourist destination. The country receives over 10 million visitors every year.

The Sahara is
the largest desert
in the world and
is bigger than
the continent of
North America.
Africa is the
world's second
driest continent
after Australia.
It is the hottest
continent on
earth too.

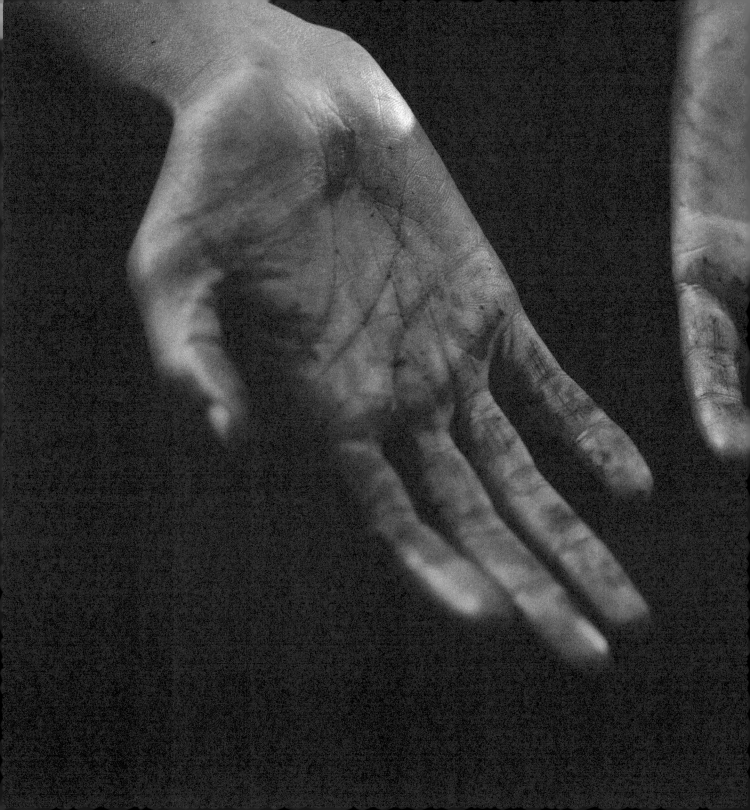

Africa has about 30% of the earth's remaining mineral resources. Nigeria is the fourth largest oil exporter in the world. Witwatersrand in South Africa produces almost half of all the gold mined in Africa.

Lake Victoria is the largest lake in Africa and the second-largest freshwater lake in the world. The longest river in the world is the Nile River with a total length of 6,650 kilometers.

Madagascar is the largest island in Africa and the fourth largest in the world. It is in the Indian Ocean off the east coast of Africa. The lemur is only found in the wild in Madagascar.

Mount
Kilimanjaro
is the highest
mountain in
Africa. It is as
high as 19,300
feet. It is so tall
that glaciers
can be found
at its summit
even though
the mountain is
near the equator.
The Chagga
people call Mt.
Kilimanjaro
home.

The Serengeti in Tanzania hosts the world's largest wildlife migration on Earth. There are over 750,000 zebra marching ahead of 1.2 million wildebeest as they cross this amazing landscape.

Africa has over 25% of the world's bird species. The word 'Africa' usually goes hand-in-hand with mental images of a vast savanna with animals of many different species living, eating, hunting, and resting.

Few people
have internet
connections in
Africa. There are
no more than 100
million Facebook
users in all of
Africa.

Africa is a home
for 167 different
species. We
should protect
their ecological
niches to keep
them from being
endangered.

Printed in the USA
CPSIA information can be obtained
at www.ICGtesting.com
CBHW061248120824
12967CB00036B/933